Riding Hood, Red Riding Hood, the wolf is prowling in the wood. Red

In this pack

Teacher's book
Ideas to help you get the most out of the story, the song and the cards.

Audio CD
Track 1
The story, with sound effects
Track 2
The song, with sound effects
Track 3
The musical accompaniment to the song
Track 4
The musical accompaniment to the song, with dance calls
Tracks 5–8
Character musical motifs
Tracks 9–12
Character movement tracks
Track 13
Forest soundtrack

Large storyline cards
Card fronts have large colour illustrations specially designed to enhance the storytelling and provide additional material for discussion. Card reverses display the poem text

Small storyline cards
Small versions of the storyline cards

Companion resources
Little Red Riding Hood wooden character set
Little Red Riding Hood interactive CD-ROM

In this book

Introduction	2
Little Red Riding Hood	5
Getting started	8
Talk about the story	10
Music and movement	12
Imagination and role play	15
Character	17
Places	18
Story and sequence	19
Sounds and words	20
Doors to further learning	22
Photocopy masters	23
Little Red Riding Hood – music	27
A simple circle dance	30
Character motifs – music	32

Introduction

Come Alive Stories is a highly flexible resource that combines story, music, movement and drama to bring a traditional tale to life. It is suitable for children from the beginning of the Foundation Stage through to Key Stage 1 across a wide range of abilities (including special educational needs) and learning styles (visual, auditory and kinaesthetic). It offers a wealth of opportunities to explore stories through play, providing a solid foundation and meaningful context for literacy activities, through a good balance of teacher-led activities and child-centred, play-based learning.

At the core of each of the *Come Alive Stories* is a traditional story, artfully retold in verse. This verse is set to music in a lively, catchy song. Both poem and song incorporate features that make them ideal for developing language skills:

- strong rhythms
- rhyme and alliteration
- repetition
- variation on familiar structure
- a chorus for joining in.

This resource offers an easy way to incorporate musical activity into young children's learning. It requires no particular musical ability – just the readiness to have some fun!

With the story as the starting point, the activities take a holistic approach to developing knowledge, skills and understanding across all areas of the Foundation Stage curriculum.[1] They support especially the area of Communication, Language and Literacy, offering opportunities to: 'share and enjoy rhymes, music, songs, poetry and stories', 'link language with physical movement in action songs and rhymes, and role-play', and 'develop a growing interest in rhyming, alliteration, sounds and words' (*Curriculum Guidance for the Foundation Stage*, DfES, 2000).

At Key Stage 1, there are opportunities for work in literacy (including shared and guided reading, identifying phonemic features, analysing and modelling story structure), and in other subjects including music, PE, geography and PSHCE.

Learning intentions are shown in this book through key references to relevant Early Learning Goals and Stepping Stones from *Curriculum Guidance for the Foundation Stage*, to Key Stage 1 National Curriculum objectives, and to literacy learning objectives within the Primary National Strategy draft renewed literacy framework.

Come Alive Stories embraces the principles of Excellence and Enjoyment in promoting vivid, enjoyable and challenging learning experiences which engage children in their learning, promote creativity and involve group interaction. The stories also provide opportunities for matching teaching techniques and strategies to a range of learning styles, enriching the learning curriculum across a number of subject areas.

Come Alive Stories follows a number of key ideas from current pedagogic thinking and research. This includes those which address concerns about children from language-poor backgrounds and, in particular, those which recognise and appreciate the important role of story, rhythm, rhyme, music and movement in the acquisition and development of children's language and literacy.

Immersion in stories:
- develops all aspects of listening
- develops imaginative engagement, especially if we can put ourselves into the story and find out what it means for us
- instils deep knowledge of story language and form, which is a prerequisite for engaging with books
- develops motivation for reading
- provides a meaningful context for role play and creative activity, which in turn increase social skills and confidence.

Curriculum Guidance for the Foundation Stage
Area of learning → ← Stepping Stone (yellow, blue or green)

CLL 7 (Reading) y1 Listen to and join in with stories and poems

Literacy Learning Objective
Core aspect of learning: speaking and listening (S&L); reading (R); writing (W)

Y1 (S&L) Retell stories, ordering events using story language

Links to curriculum guidance will be updated in line with changes to the national frameworks.

Visit **www.yellow-door.net** and click on downloads.

Immersion in rhythm and rhyme:
- underpins both phonological and phonemic awareness
- develops children's ability to hear pitch and feel the beat – keeping a steady beat or 'beat competency' is thought to be one of the best predictors of later academic success
- develops sensitivity to the patterns of language, and especially to the patterns of written forms.

Music is a natural form of communication for children and has been shown to:
- develop auditory memory
- be emotionally satisfying
- contribute significantly to later reading ability
- develop a healthy group dynamic, which in turn creates an environment that invites sharing.

Kinaesthetic activities (including the dramatic arts) have been shown to:
- facilitate academic readiness and learning
- lead to improvements in children emotionally, physically and cognitively
- help integrate different parts of the mind and body (through Brain Gym® type activities), leading to improvements in self-esteem and the ability to focus on a task.

The activities in *Come Alive Stories* tap into these aspects of story, rhythm and rhyme, and music and movement. They are aimed at developing these underpinning skills and concepts, as well as creating the sort of engagement with stories and music that will lead children into enjoyment, creativity and storytelling.

[1] For a clear overview of this approach, see Sue Palmer and Ros Bayley, 2004, *Foundations of Literacy*, Network Educational Press.

Little Red Riding Hood

The elements of Little Red Riding Hood (a girl confronting a wolf) are found in traditional stories from around the world, but the European story that we know today was popularised by the brothers Grimm in the nineteenth century. They remodelled the tale from earlier Italian and French versions, leaving out some of the more unpalatable features! The brothers Grimm introduced the red hood (or *Rotkäppchen*), which is thought to have been inspired by the red caps worn by girls during church feast days in the villages where the brothers lived.

1
There was a girl, or so it's said,
Who had a lovely cloak of red.
She wore it everywhere she could,
So she was called Red Riding Hood.

One afternoon she planned to go
And visit Grandma, on her own.
Now Grandma had a house that stood
Alone inside the nearby wood.

Her mother said, "Be very good,"
And handed to Red Riding Hood,
A basket full of cakes and bread.
"Take this to Grandma, please," she said.

Red Riding Hood, Red Riding Hood,
The wolf is prowling in the wood.
Red Riding Hood, Red Riding Hood,
He'd eat you if he could.

2

A little way along the trail,
She met a stranger with a tail.
"Good day," he said. "Now tell me where
You're going with that basket there."

"I'm going to visit Grandmamma.
It's through the wood, and not so far."
She pointed out the path ahead.
"How kind!" the hairy stranger said.

Red Riding Hood went on her way.
The wolf pretended he would stay,
Then took a shortcut through the trees,
And got to Grandma's first, with ease.

Red Riding Hood, Red Riding Hood,
The wolf is prowling in the wood.
Red Riding Hood, Red Riding Hood,
He'd eat you if he could.

3

The wolf found Grandma tucked in bed.
"I'm going to eat you up," he said.
"Oh dear," she cried. "Well, do your worst,"
"But you will have to catch me first!"

She leapt from bed, she ran straight past,
And nipped into the wardrobe, fast.
Her cap and shawl fell as she ran,
Which gave the wolf a cunning plan.

He wriggled into Grandma's clothes,
Then cleared his throat and wiped his nose.
And when Red Riding Hood came in,
He greeted her with toothy grin.

Red Riding Hood, Red Riding Hood,
The wolf is prowling in the wood.
Red Riding Hood, Red Riding Hood,
He'd eat you if he could.

4

"Oh Grandmamma, what great big eyes!"
The girl remarked, with some surprise.
"All the better to see you, dear,"
The wolf replied. "Come over here."

"Oh Grandmamma, what great big ears!"
The girl remarked, while drawing near.
"All the better to hear you, dear,"
The wolf replied. "Please, have no fear."

"Oh Grandmamma, what great big teeth!"
The girl remarked and took a seat.
"All the better to EAT you, dear!"
The wolf replied. His plan was clear.

Red Riding Hood, Red Riding Hood,
The wolf is prowling in the wood.
Red Riding Hood, Red Riding Hood,
He'd eat you if he could.

5

The wolf drew near, his eyes agleam.
Red Riding Hood let out a scream.
As luck would have it, passing by,
A wandering woodsman heard her cry.

He dashed in through the open door,
He shook his axe and gave a roar.
The wolf complained, "You've spoilt my plan!"
He tore off all the clothes, and ran.

Then from the wardrobe Grandma burst,
A bit surprised, but none the worse.
So as the clock was striking three,
They all sat down to cakes and tea.

Red Riding Hood, Red Riding Hood,
The wolf's no longer in the wood.
Red Riding Hood, Red Riding Hood,
The wolf is gone for good!

Retold by Debbie Pullinger

Red Riding Hood, Red Riding Hood, the wolf is prowling in the wood. Red Riding Hood, Red Riding

Getting started

CLL2 (Comm.) ELG4 Listen with enjoyment to stories, songs, rhymes and poems and respond with relevant comments, questions and actions

CLL 7 (Reading) y1 Listen to and join in with stories and poems
CLL2 (Comm.) y1 Join in with repeated refrains, anticipating key events and important phrases

Enjoy the poem

Read the poem aloud yourself or listen together to the reading on the audio CD. Show the illustrations on the large storyline cards. You could either peg the cards on a washing line after each one is read, or ask children to hold them. The poem text is printed on the reverse so you can read the text whilst showing the card. You might want to point to the characters as they are mentioned to focus the children's attention. Use plenty of eye contact and expression to draw the children into the story.

During the reading of the story and subsequent discussion, the set of small storyline cards can be particularly valuable for use with children with special educational needs: a child can be given their own set of pictures to look at, perhaps with the support of a learning assistant.

Clap and chant

Encourage the children to join in with the refrain. Ask them to emphasise the words **Riding**, **wolf** and **eat** to help them to pick up the rhythm.

Children could then clap the pulse as they chant. They could try using horizontal (normal) clapping for the Red Riding Hood lines, and vertical clapping (hands moving up and down like the wolf's jaws) for the wolf lines.

Make sure they understand the meaning of **prowling**; you could ask for demonstrations!

Riding Hood, Red Riding Hood, the wolf is prowling in the wood. Red Riding Hood, Red Riding Hoo

Sing the song

When the children are familiar with the poem and story, they will be ready to hear the song. If they have been chanting the refrain, they will be able to join in with these straight away. As they become familiar with the melody, encourage them to sing the verses as well. They could begin by joining in with the parts where the characters speak – using suitable voices and expression. Don't worry at this stage about whether they are pitching the notes accurately – involvement is the important thing! Continue clapping the pulse, as above, in the refrains.

CD2 (Music) y1 Join in favourite songs

Music 1 a) Use voices expressively by singing songs and speaking chants and rhymes

Talk about the pictures

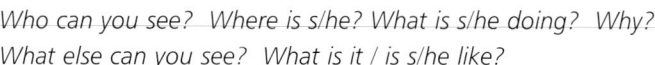

Begin with a general discussion about the story and progress to talking about individual pictures to aid comprehension. Move from the obvious to the detailed and then to the inferred. Ask questions for each picture, such as:

Who can you see? Where is s/he? What is s/he doing? Why?
What else can you see? What is it / is s/he like?

Ask particularly if they can see the wolf in picture 1. What is he doing? What is he going to do?

Sequence the story

The cards can be used for sequencing, including chronological ordering, with opportunities for using vocabulary such as:

First … Next … Then … Finally …

You can also use the cards to ask:

What happened next? Which card shows …?

CLL7 (Reading) ELG1 Retell narratives in the correct sequence, drawing on language patterns of stories

Y1 (S&L) Retell stories, ordering events using story language
Y2 (S&L) Tell real and imagined stories using the conventions of familiar story language

9

Red Riding Hood, Red Riding Hood, the wolf is prowling in the wood. Red Riding Hood, Red Riding

Talk about the story

CLL3(Comm) ELG Extend vocabulary, exploring the meanings and sounds of new words

Words and language

A verse-by-verse reading of the poem can lead to more detailed observation and discussion, including an explanation of any unfamiliar words such as **short-cut**, **nipped**, **remarked**. Ask children who they think 'the hairy stranger' is, and what is meant by the clock 'striking three'.

With older Key Stage 1 children, a simple glossary could be made.

CLL7 (Reading) ELG 5 Show an understanding of the elements of stories, such as main character, sequence of events and openings

KS1 Geography 2a Use geographical vocabulary [e.g., hill, river, motorway, near, far, north, south]

The settings

This story has two scenes:

- **Scene 1: the edge of the forest.** Using pictures 1 and 2, look at the main geographical features: hills, fields, trees, bushes and paths. Talk about the landscape and how it is different from or similar to where the children live or places they have visited. Discuss the different types of plants which grow in a forest; what else might be living there? (Small animals, such as insects; larger animals; birds.) Listen to the forest soundtrack on the CD. Children could close their eyes and imagine the scene.

- **Scene 2: Grandma's bedroom.** Look at the furniture in the bedroom: how is it similar to or different from what the children have in their bedrooms? Talk about the furnishings: wardrobe, clock, bedspread, etc. When do they think this story took place (long ago), and why? Think about the sounds for picture 5; what would you hear? The list could include: the woodsman's roar, the wolf complaining 'You've spoilt my plan', Grandma's 'Ooh!' of surprise, and the clock striking three.

10

You could ask individual children to make these sounds (perhaps identifying those children with accessories, as described on page 16) then ask the others to put the children representing the sounds into the correct order.

Explore the story

To reinforce each character's role in the story, ask about their actions, and relate this to vocabulary from the poem. You could ask, for example:

Who prowled? Who leapt and nipped?

Use individual pictures to discuss what happens to the characters:

Picture 1: Red Riding Hood, her mother, the wolf (in the trees)
Picture 2: Red Riding Hood, the wolf – *Now where do they go?* (Red Riding hood on the main path, the wolf along implied path through the trees)
Picture 3: Grandma, the wolf – *What's happened to Grandma's cap?*
Picture 4: The wolf, Red Riding Hood – *Where's Grandma?*
Picture 5: The woodsman, the wolf, Grandma – *Now where does the wolf go?*

Extend the discussion by exploring motives. This could lead to wider discussions about the children's own behaviour. You could ask:

Why did Red Riding Hood …
… take food to Grandma? (How can we look after older members of our families?)
… talk to the stranger in the wood? (What should she have done? What would you do if you were approached by a stranger?)

Why did …
… Grandma hide in the wardrobe?
… they all sit down for cakes and tea? (Where did the cakes come from?)

CLL5 (Thinking) ELG 8 Use talk to organise, sequence and clarify thinking, ideas, feelings and events
CLL2 (Comm.) ELG 2 Sustain attentive listening, responding to what they have heard by relevant comments, questions or actions

Y1 (S&L) Ask and answer questions, make relevant contributions, offer suggestions and take turns
Y1 (R) Make predictions, showing an understanding of ideas, events and characters

PSED4 ELG2 Consider the consequences of their words and actions for themselves & others

KS1 PSHCE 4d That family and friends should care for each other

Music and movement

CD2 (Music) y2 Show interest in how musical instruments sound

The poem has been set to music in the form of a traditional English jig, played in a folk-rock style and with four special instruments to listen for. Each of these instruments represents one of the main characters and has its own tune – or 'motif' – which you will hear as that character is introduced into the story. They are:

Red Riding Hood: flute

The wolf: accordion

Grandma: violin

The woodsman: French horn

Once they have listened to the song, children will be able to sing and play along, either to the sung version or (when the words and tune are reasonably well known) to the instrumental version. The song could eventually provide the basis for a performance of some kind, perhaps involving actions.

CD2 (Music) b3 Tap out simple repeated rhythms
CD2 (Music) g2 Explore the different sounds of instruments

KS 1 Music 1 b) Play tuned and untuned instruments
KS1 Music 4 c) How sounds can be made in different ways [e.g. vocalising, clapping, by musical instruments]

Listen to the instruments

Play the musical motif tracks and challenge children to match the tunes to the characters and/or to the instruments – you could show pictures of the instruments (you could use the ones on page 25) or, better still, real instruments. Discuss what the instruments are made of and how they are played (flute and French horn are blown; the violin is bowed; on the accordion, pulling and pushing the bellows and pressing the buttons pushes air through reeds).

The following rhymes, adapted from the poem, each follow the rhythm of that character's musical motif. Chanting the rhymes will help the children to hear the melodies of the musical motifs.

Red Riding Hood, Red Riding Hood,
The wolf is prowling in the wood.
Red Riding Hood, Red Riding Hood,
He'd eat you if he could.

The wolf, the wolf,
The wolf is prowling in the wood.
The wolf, the wolf,
He'd eat you if he could.

Grandma, Grandma,
Grandma,
Grandma,
He'd eat you if he could.

The woodsman,
The woodsman,
The wolf is gone for good!

Chant the rhymes as a group, then sing along with the motifs. (The music for these is on page 32.) All the melodies are within a chord of G which can be made with three chime bars: G B and D:

Red Riding Hood: **G B B B**   The wolf: **B D**
Grandma: **G G**   The woodsman: **G D D**

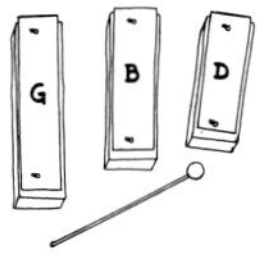

To introduce each melody, you could listen to the note on which it begins. The rhythm for each will come naturally from saying the words. You could then play the melodies to the children and ask which characters they represent.

Make the chime bars available on a music table, and encourage the children to try playing the names. Older Key Stage 1 children may be able to play them on a recorder or other instrument. Once they have identified these tunes, encourage children to listen for them in the sung and instrumental versions.

Move to the music

The children will probably want to clap along and maybe dance. Some will naturally skip or gallop to the beat, so let them enjoy moving to the music. Then begin to relate the movement to the story and to the principal character in each verse:

Verse 1: Red Riding Hood (skipping)
Verse 2: The wolf (prowling – big steps)
Verse 3: Grandma (little steps)

2, 3, 9–12
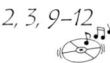

PD 1 (Movement) y2 Respond to rhythm, music & story by means of gesture and movement
CD 2 (Music) b5 Imitate & create movement in response to music

Verse 4: The wolf as Grandma (delicate big steps!)
Verse 5: The woodsman (striding)

Encourage creativity and expression to enact each part of the story through movement. For the refrains, stop and clap in the way suggested on page 8. This work could be developed into a more formal dance, as described in the next section.

A simple circle dance

CD2 (Music) y4 Enjoy joining in with dancing & ring games
PD 2 (Movement) y2 Combine & repeat a range of movements
KS1 PE 6c Create and perform dances using simple movement patterns

This circle dance, appropriate to the English folk-dance style of the music, can be done with any number of children; a class-sized group of 12 to 30 would be most suitable. You will need a reasonably large space such as a school hall. See page 30 for illustrated instructions. These can be used in conjunction with track 4 on the audio CD, which has the music together with called directions. Once the dance has been learned, you could use the music on track 3.

Mood music

Y2 (S&L) Consider how mood and atmosphere are created through live or recorded performance

KS1 Music 2 b) Explore, choose and organise sounds and musical ideas.
KS1 Music 4 c) How sounds can be made in different ways [for example, vocalising, clapping, by musical instruments, in the environment]

Make your own forest music. Use classroom instruments and the children's voices to create a piece of forest music or 'sound picture'.

You could start by listening to the forest soundtrack and discussing what other noises might be heard in the forest, then asking the children to suggest how they could make those noises; for example: the wind in the trees (shakers), insects (scrapers), animals, birds (voices), stream (rain stick).

Then, with the children in different groups for different sound effects, you (or a child) could conduct the sound picture by pointing to each group, indicating volume by raising or lowering your arm. Begin with one section (such as the wind) and build up the picture gradually, perhaps as you describe the forest coming to life in the early morning. A large suspended cymbal hit harder and harder with small fast strokes using soft beaters could signify the sunrise.

Imagination and role play

Little Red Riding Hood provides lots of opportunities for imaginative role play and for exploring the question of how to assume a character.

Playing a role

Explore with the children how the wolf pretended to be someone else (Grandma):

- **He changed his appearance** – by wearing Grandma's clothes. (Did that really make him look like Grandma?) Ask the children what they would use to make themselves look like the characters in the story. You could make dressing-up resources and accessories available.
- **He changed his voice** – to sound like Grandma's voice. How do little girls talk? How do grandmas talk? What about wolves in stories? Encourage the children to try speaking like the different characters. Use the speech from the story, perhaps using lines written in speech bubbles.
- **He moved differently** – like Grandma. Try moving like the different characters. For example: skip like Red Riding Hood, prowl like the wolf, stride like the woodsman, hobble like Grandma. Older children could think about how a grandma would 'leap' and 'nip'.
- **He changed position** – moving into the place where Grandma would have been (the bed). Relate this to the children's own experiences: for example, if a child were pretending to be the teacher, would it help to sit in the teacher's chair? Or to stand where the teacher stands? You could ask children to try this out!

CLL5 (Thinking) ELG7 Use language to imagine & recreate roles
CD3 (Imagination) b2 Use available resources to create props to support role play

Y1 (S&L) Explore familiar themes and characters through improvisation and role play
Y1 (R) Visualise and comment on events, characters and ideas, making imaginative links to own experience
Y2 (S&L) Give reasons for why things happen or characters change

Act out the story

CD3 (Imagination) g3 Play co-operatively as part of a group to act out a narrative

Y1 (S&L) Act out own and well-known stories, using voices for characters

Y2 (S&L) Adopt appropriate roles; present traditional stories

Use the discussion about playing a role as a stimulus for free play based on the story. Use a suitable setting: perhaps a home corner set out as Grandma's bedroom, or next to a forest frieze. Encourage the children to act in role, using voice, facial expression and movement as well as the props. You could begin by retelling the story, and then encourage children to develop their own stories. You could suggest that they introduce a different character into the action to change the storyline. You or another adult may wish to support this. Simple 'accessories' could be used to identify the characters, for example:

- Red Riding Hood: red cloak or headscarf
- Grandma: mob-cap (a suitable shower cap would work well!)
- Mother: apron
- Wolf: headband with ears
- Woodsman: 'Robin Hood'-type hat (could be made from folded paper)

In the hot seat

CLL5 (Thinking) ELG 7 Use language to imagine and recreate roles

Create character profiles by compiling a word list for each character, then use the lists in a hot-seat activity. Play 'Who is it?' games by asking, for example: 'I'm thinking of a character who …' (clues could include words, movements or objects).

Small-world play

CLL2 (Comm.) ELG1 Enjoy listening to and using spoken language and readily turn to it in their play and learning

Wooden or other model characters can be used for table-top storytelling. Alternatively, make stick puppets using the character pictures on page 23 copied onto card and coloured by the children. Encourage the children to attribute voices, emotions and actions to the figures. You or the children could create story settings, such as a class-frieze backdrop of woods and cottages.

Character

Features – Oh Grandmamma!

In the story, Red Riding Hood notices the wolf's eyes, ears and teeth, and the wolf in turn points out what each of these is used for. This could link to science work on 'ourselves' and our senses. Talk about what we use our eyes, ears and teeth for. Discuss the fact that animals also have these features, but that they may look different from human features. Consider the difference between a wolf's eyes, ears and teeth and human eyes, ears and teeth. How else are wolves different from humans?

Explore the children's understanding of other senses or features by making up more lines for Red Riding Hood, for example:

Oh Grandmamma, what a great big nose!

You could use this as an opportunity to explore how differences in appearance can be used negatively. Discuss how sometimes we laugh at people or call them names, or make them feel bad, just because they are different in some way. Reinforce the concept of mutual respect.

PSED4 ELG2 Consider the consequences of their words and actions for themselves & others
PSED2 ELG2 Have a developing awareness of their own ... views & feelings, and be sensitive to those of others

KS1 PSHCE 4e That there are different types of teasing and bullying
KS1Sc2 2a Recognise and compare the main external parts of the bodies of humans and other animals
KS1Sc2 2g About the senses that enable humans and other animals to be aware of the world around them
KS1Sc2 4a Recognise similarities and differences between themselves and others, and to treat others with sensitivity

Feelings

Encourage the children to consider how the characters felt at various points during the story. When have the children felt scared, brave, surprised, etc.?

Character profiles

Create character profile sheets, using the pictures from page 23.* These may be completed either as a class or individual activity, using vocabulary from the story or the children's own words. Children can be encouraged to write a sentence or two about the character and/or add speech or thought in a bubble.

CLL8 (Writing) ELG2 Attempt writing for various purposes

Y1 (W) Use words and phrases, including story language
Y1 (W) Compose and write simple sentences to communicate meaning

* If you have the CD-ROM, you could use the character profiles and character sheets within the Teacher Resources.

Places

 Following discussion about settings (p.10) ask the children to consider where the places in the story are in relation to each other. Use the plan on page 26 as a basis for discussion. Relate this to the children's own area and places they know. For example, where is their house in relation to the school and how do they get there (in terms of directions)? You could use other examples such as places around the school. Ask them how they get to *their* grandma's house (or the house of another relative or friend). Discuss how we get to places and how else Red Riding Hood could have travelled.

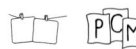

K&U 6 (Place) ELG1 observe, find out & identify features in the place they live & the natural world

Y1 (W) Convey information in simple non-narrative forms
Y1 (W) Group written sentences in chunks of meaning
KS1 Geog 2a Use geographical vocabulary [e.g., hill, river, motorway, near, far, north, south]
KS1 Geog 2e Make maps and plans [for example, a pictorial map of a place in a story].

Route planning and story-maps

Extend this into a map-drawing exercise, with the path though the woods as the storyline. You could begin by attaching the large storyline cards to a whiteboard, flipchart or large piece of paper. Ask the children what would link the pictures, and draw the pathway – leading from Red Riding Hood's cottage.

Children could then make their own story-maps using the line versions of cards 1, 2 and 3 on pages 24–25. They could stick these onto a large sheet and draw the pathway between pictures 1 and 2, and 2 and 3. They could then write words or sentences below each one to tell the story.

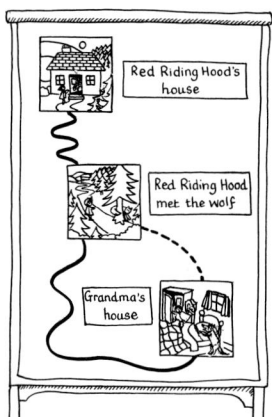

What else was there? You could use this as an opportunity to discuss geographical features. Allow the children to suggest and add other features to their map, such as hills, mountains, streams, and bridges. This could lead to other map-drawing exercises, relating to the children's houses and the route to school.

Story and sequence

The concept of story structure and chronology can be introduced in a way appropriate to age and key stage.

Ask the children to think about the plot in terms of place, chronology, character and action.

Picture	1	2	3	4	5
Where	The edge of the wood		Grandma's house		
When	First	Then	Next	After that	Finally / in the end
Who	RRH (and mother)	Wolf	Grandma	Wolf dressed as Grandma	Woodsman
What	Mother asks RRH to take basket	RRH meets the wolf	Wolf takes Grandma's place in bed	Wolf talks to RRH	Woodsman chases wolf away

You could ask the children to tell the story using only a title plus five key words – one for each of the pictures. The words could be five names or five objects (e.g. basket, woods, bed, wardrobe, clock). This could be extended for older children to five phrases or five sentences to tell the story.

Making storybooks

Use the line versions of the illustrations on pages 24–25 to make five-page zig-zag books. Children can use the space below the pictures to add labels or speech bubbles or write their own version of the story. Alternatively, provide five blank pages which can be used for retelling the story through drawing or emergent writing.

Y1 (R) Recognise the main elements that shape different texts
Y1 (W) Use key features of narrative in their writing
Y1 (W) Group written sentences in chunks of meaning

Y1 (W) Use words and phrases including story language
Y1 (W) Compose and write simple sentences to communicate meaning

Sounds and words

CLL2 (Comm.) ELG Extend vocabulary, exploring the meanings and sounds of new words
CLL6 (Sounds & letters) ELG2 Link sounds to letters
Missing rhymes
CLL7 (Reading) ELG1 Explore and experiment with sounds, words and texts

Y1 (R) Explore the effect of patterns of language and repeated words

Little Red Riding Hood offers many opportunities for developing both phonological and, later, phonemic awareness. The verse contains the following rhymes:

said / red / bread / ahead / bed
could / hood / stood / wood / good
trail / tail
where / there
Grandmamma / far
way / stay
trees / ease
worst / first
past / fast
ran / plan

in / grin
eyes / surprise
dear / here / ear(s) / near / fear / clear
agleam / scream
by / cry
door / roar
three / tea

Children may suggest **go/own**, **clothes/nose**, **burst/worse**, **teeth/seat** as rhyming pairs. They could be discussed as half rhymes or 'near rhymes': the vowel sounds are the same and the end-sounds of the words are similar but not exactly the same. For older children, word-level work can be related to the written letter patterns, with children noticing where the same sounds are spelled differently (e.g. **said**, **bread**, **bed**).

Missing rhymes

CLL6 (Sounds & Letters) g1
Continue a rhyming string

Even when the story is still relatively unfamiliar, the children should be able to predict many of the rhymes. Read a couplet, raising your voice in anticipation as you approach the final word, but leaving it out so the children can supply it, for example:

*Red Riding Hood, Red Riding Hood,
The wolf is prowling in the …*

Then take away one of the context clues (the first line) but again use rhythm to structure and prompt the response, for example:

> Think of a word that rhymes with **hood**.
> The wolf is prowling in the …

Then progress to taking away the poem line altogether, for example:

> Think of a word that rhymes with **hood**.
> **Hood** … and …

Encourage the children to think of as many other rhyming words as they can, for example **stood** and **good**.

This could lead to children composing whole lines of their own. For example:

> Red Riding Hood, Red Riding Hood,
> Don't talk to strangers in the wood.

or

> Red Riding Hood, Red Riding Hood,
> Just run away – you know you should!

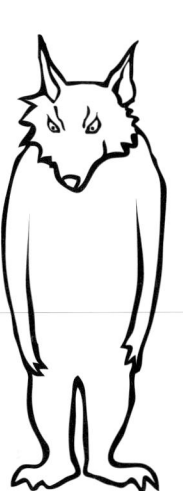

Spot the mistake

When children know the story well, put in a wrong word at the end of a rhyming pair. Ask them to spot it, and supply the right word.

Rhyming pairs

For older children, give each child a card with one of the rhyming words from the poem. Everyone walks around the room saying their word, looking for their rhyming partners. When they have found them, the pair look at their words together. Encourage them to look at what is the same and what is different.

Doors to further learning

Little Red Riding Hood offers lots of opportunities to link other areas of learning and the curriculum.

- Do a 'five senses' quiz, where children have to use each of their senses to identify different objects (e.g. a hairbrush in a feely bag, some vinegar in a jar, an audio recording of a car). Discuss how they could tell what the objects were, and where the sense organs are in the body. Look at photographs of animals and compare the different sizes and shapes of eyes, ears, noses.

- Make a table-top model forest. Make trees out of cardboard rolls, cutting slits in the top and bending back to make branches, then make paper leaves to stick on the ends. Make Red Riding Hood's house and Grandma's house from cardboard boxes. Arrange the forest and the houses, create pathways though the forest, and add wooden or cardboard story characters. Children could draw their own maps of the model forest.

- Children could use mirrors to look at their own teeth and the different shapes. Look at the sharp teeth at the front for biting and the flat teeth at the back for chewing and grinding.

- Plan and then have Red Riding Hood's tea party, to include cakes and bread (perhaps sandwiches, cut into different shapes). You could make small cakes and decorate them to look like the faces of the story characters.

- Talk about the types of plants and animals you might find in a forest or woodland habitat – for example: different sorts of trees, birds, mammals, insects and other mini-beasts. If possible, go on a woodland walk. Listen to the sounds you can hear in the wood or forest. Take bark or leaf rubbings. Collect twigs, leaves, pine cones, acorns and other natural objects for a classroom display. Sort the leaves by shape, size and colour.

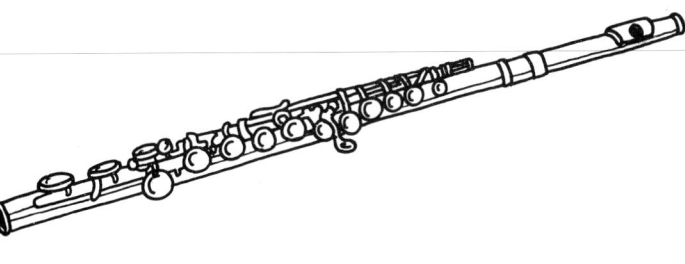

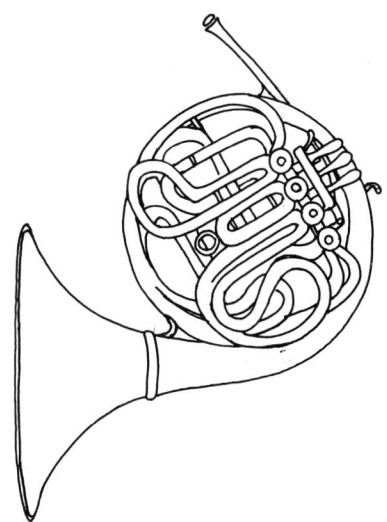

Little Red Riding Hood – music

Composed by Tim Harding

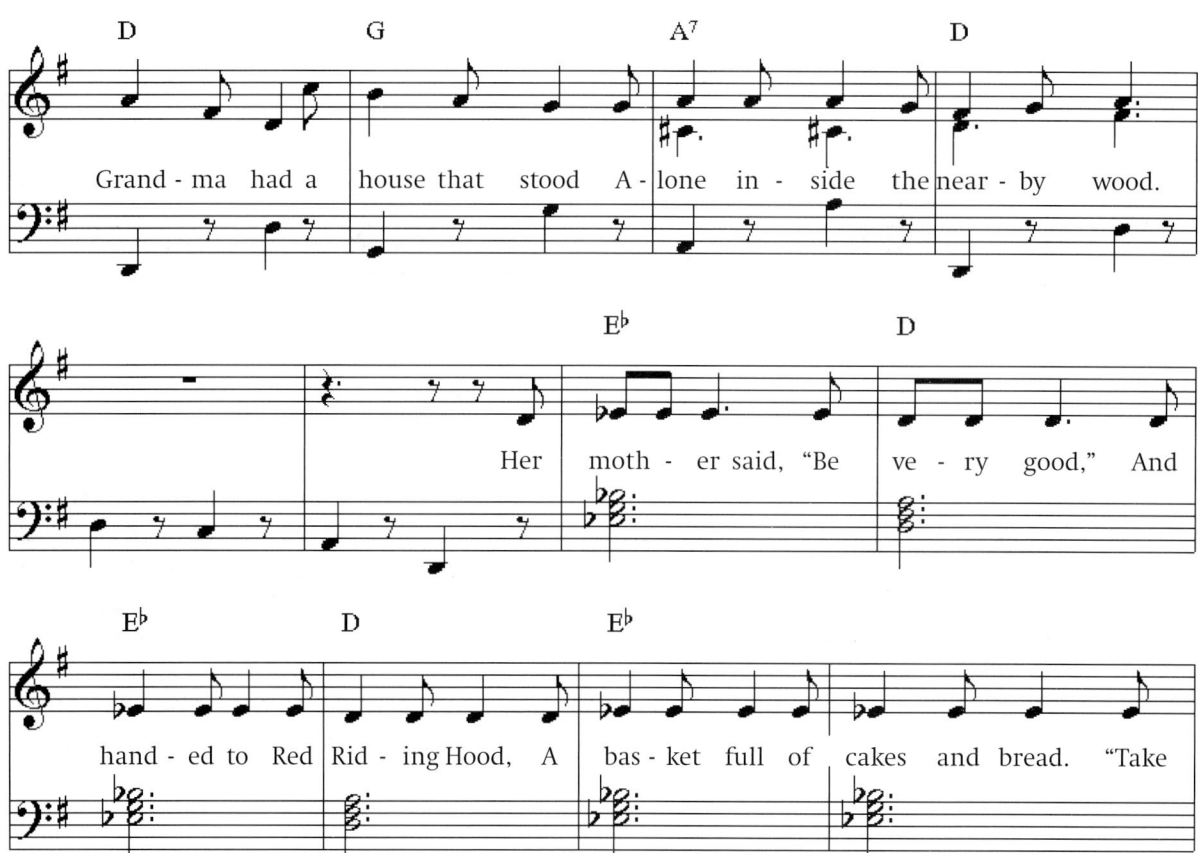

A simple circle dance

Before the dance begins, choose individual children to be Red Riding Hood, the wolf, Grandma, mother and the woodsman. It will be helpful to identify these children in some way, perhaps using accessories as suggested on page 16.

Each section of the dance corresponds to a section of music; so for each verse there are three main sections or 'stanzas' and a chorus. When children clap the chorus they could use horizontal (normal) clapping for the Red Riding Hood lines, and vertical clapping (hands moving up and down like the wolf's jaws) for the wolf lines. Walk the dance through slowly, verse by verse, before attempting the whole dance with the music.

Verse 1
Intro All hold hands in circle; RRH and mother to middle of circle and hold two hands.

S1 All circle left (walk or gallop); RRH and mother dance round each other.

S2 All circle right; RRH and mother dance round each other the other way.

S3 All circle raise hands like trees; RRH skips in and out of the trees around the circle; mother stays in middle waving.

Chorus All (including RRH and mother) stand in circle and clap.

Verse 2
Intro All hold hands in circle; RRH and wolf to middle of circle and hold two hands.

S1 All circle left; RRH and wolf dance round each other.

S2 All circle right; RRH and wolf dance round each other the other way.

S3 All circle raise hands like trees; RRH skips in and out of the trees around the circle; wolf follows RRH, then cuts across middle of circle.

Chorus All (including RRH and wolf) stand in circle and clap.

Verse 3

Intro All hold hands in circle; wolf and Grandma to middle of circle and hold two hands.

S1 All circle left; wolf and Grandma dance round each other.

S2 All circle right; wolf and Grandma dance round each other the other way.

S3 All hold hands in circle; Grandma ducks under hands and skips round the outside of circle; wolf stays in middle, prowling.

Chorus All (including wolf and Grandma) stand in circle and clap.

Verse 4

Intro All hold hands in circle; RRH and wolf to middle of circle and hold two hands.

S1 All circle left; RRH and wolf dance round each other.

S2 All circle right; RRH and wolf dance round each other the other way.

S3 All hold hands and move into middle of circle and out again; RRH and wolf stay in centre.

Chorus All (including RRH and wolf) stand in circle and clap.

Verse 5

Intro All hold hands in circle; RRH and wolf to middle of circle and hold two hands.

S1 All circle left; RRH and wolf dance round each other.

S2 All circle right; woodsman joins RRH and wolf in centre and all three dance round each other.

S3 All hold hands; wolf ducks under hands and skips round outside of circle.

Chorus RRH and woodsman are joined by Grandma in middle and all three circle left; all others stand in circle and clap.
Repeated chorus Continue clapping; three in middle circle right.

Character motifs – music

Composed by Tim Harding